Real Estate Investing:

The Ultimate Wealth Guide to Rental Property Investing, Real Estate & Passive Income

By Lara Jaidyn

© Copyright 2016 - All rights reserved.

In no way is it legal to reproduce, duplicate, or transmit any part of this document in either electronic means or in printed format. Recording of this publication is strictly prohibited and any storage of this document is not allowed unless with written permission from the publisher. All rights reserved.

The information provided herein is stated to be truthful and consistent, in that any liability, in terms of inattention or otherwise, by any usage or abuse of any policies, processes, or directions contained within is the solitary and utter responsibility of the recipient reader. Under no circumstances will any legal responsibility or blame be held against the publisher for any reparation, damages, or monetary loss due to the information herein, either directly or indirectly. Respective authors own all copyrights not held by the publisher.

Legal Notice:

This book is copyright protected. This is only for personal use. You cannot amend, distribute, sell, use, quote or paraphrase any part or the content within this book without the consent of the author or copyright owner. Legal action will be pursued if this is breached.

Disclaimer Notice:

Please note the information contained within this document is for educational and entertainment purposes only. Every attempt has been made to provide accurate, up to date and reliable complete information. No warranties of any kind are expressed or implied. Readers acknowledge that the author is not engaging in the rendering of legal, financial, medical or professional advice.

By reading this document, the reader agrees that under no circumstances are we responsible for any losses, direct or indirect, which are incurred as a result of the use of information contained within this document, including, but not limited to; errors, omissions, or inaccuracies.

Table of Contents

Introduction 1

Chapter 1: What Is Passive Income? 3

Chapter 2: Are You Cut Out to Be a Landlord? 6

Chapter 5: Things You Need to Know About Financing an Investment Property 15

Chapter 6: Purchasing Your Property – The Real Estate Agent 19

Chapter 7: Purchasing Your Property – The Offer 22

Chapter 8: Getting Ready to Find a Renter 24

Chapter 9: Selecting A Renter 31

Chapter 10: Protecting Yourself, Your Property, and Your Tenant . 42

Chapter 11: The Rehabilitation of Rental Properties 47

Chapter 12: The Four Core Exiting Strategies 49

Chapter 13: Extra Information and Terms 53

Chapter 14: The Fundamentals of Being a Successful Property Investor/Manager 57

Conclusion 60

Introduction

Congratulations, I would like to thank you for downloading my book, *Real Estate Investing: The Ultimate Wealth Guide to Rental Property Investing, Real Estate & Passive Income.*

Chances are, you have picked up this book because you have an avid interest in investing in rental income; but aren't sure where to get started. Yes, investing in real estate is a great idea; especially if you are looking for a 'sure' way to create passive income.

However, as you may probably already know, investing in real estate isn't as easy as going out and buying a house to rent out to people. In fact, there are many intricate steps and considerations involved in the entire process, and that is where this book is going assist you. So, you can succeed in the property investment world, too.

So, as soon as you have made the decision to invest in rental property, you are probably going to want to go right out and start looking for a house to invest in. But, before you start calling real estate agents, there are a few things that I want you to know about.

Some of the things you are going to want to research include:

1. The type of property you are going to invest in.
2. How much you can afford to pay.
3. What neighborhoods you may want to invest in.
4. What the average rent is in that area or location.
5. How to find available houses to suit your needs.
6. How to find suitable tenants that will not let you down.
7. What kind of return you are hoping to make on your investment, exponentially.

This book is going to cover all of the topics above, as well as some other important factors that are super important to know about, *before* you begin investing.

So, please don't allow all of the topics in this book to discourage you. This book is purposefully laid out in easy to read chapters, that are going to leave you with a great understanding of property investing. You will know exactly what the first steps are, as you venture into the world of property investment and management.

Chapter 1: What Is Passive Income?

You have probably already heard that investing in real estate property is a great way to create a passive income. But what exactly is passive income? Many people incorrectly assume that passive income means - that there is never going to be any real work involved on their part. This isn't completely accurate. And let's be honest, no true investment is super easy.

The IRS defines passive income as, "net rental income and income from a business in which the taxpayer does not materially participate."

So, when you are earning a passive income, it means that you are going to be getting paid whether you actually do any meaningful work, or not. However, it doesn't mean that you never do any work, though. There can be a lot of work that needs to be done 'up front,' in order to get the ball rolling. Once that happens, it is a process of ongoing management. This is executed in an organized way, so that the workload is very manageable and also successful.

Alright, so there are some other things about passive income that you should know about in order to clear up any misconceptions you might have. This is important for your own understanding, from a law necessity view point.

What Passive Income is Not:

1. Passive income is not a one-time lump sum, like an inheritance.
2. Passive income does not mean that there is a permanent income.
3. Passive income is not 100% secure.
4. Passive income is not completely maintenance free.

What Passive Income Is:

1. Passive income is a source of revenue with some continuity.
2. All forms of passive income can eventually come to an end for various reasons.

How Do Rental Investments Create Passive Income?

Alright, so rental investments are one of the more common forms of passive income. They aren't as definitively passive as some of the other options of passive income though.

When you do invest in rental properties, you are likely going to have to do some upfront work, to get your property ready to be rented out. When your property is ready to be rented out, this doesn't mean that your job is done, however. You will need to find the tenants, and if something happens to the house; you are going to have to ensure that you are available. You will need to be there to correct the issue; or the problems that have occurred.

The great news is that when you do find tenants - they are going to be paying you a monthly rental fee. So, this fee is going to be higher than what the expenses are, of owning the house. So, this is where your rental income is going to come from. The extra funds, over and above the expenditure, fundamentally.

This revenue is not always 100% secure, as you are relying on others. They ensure that they are paying their rent every month, in order for you to make money. So, if for some reason your tenant stops making their payments. For example, they move out of the property, then you aren't going to make an income (until you have found new tenants).

Additionally, owning the investment property doesn't necessarily mean that you are going to have to be the one who is available to the tenants, in the case of an emergency. You also have the selective option to have a business partner, or an employee who is going to manage the property for you. This can take out some of the stress as well.

Remember, owning an investment property is not a get rich quick scheme. If you are looking for something that is going to earn you a lot of money quickly, this is not what you are going to want to invest in. This is a slower, steady and progressive income alternative.

In the beginning, while your tenants are paying rent, that rent payment is going to be necessary for you to pay: the mortgage, property taxes, insurance payments and any additional breakages or repairs. As the mortgage is paid off, you are going to earn more and more for yourself. This is the featured highlight, that makes it truly worthwhile.

Now that you have a good idea of what passive income is, and how it applies to rental properties, we are ready to start looking into how you can get started. We can shift our focus to actually making your passive income, from a great rental property investment.

Chapter 2: Are You Cut Out to Be a Landlord?

You may have already decided that you like the idea of creating some passive income, and you are sure that you want to take the definitive route of investment properties. However, let's make sure that you are clear on a few things, before you make the final decision and jump in with both feet, first. Because there are actually a few aspects to being a landlord, that you should definitely take into important, well thought out consideration. Let's discuss them now.

Do You Enjoy Doing Things Yourself?

When you are first starting out, you are likely not going to be able to afford to hire people to take care of the maintenance. This will be in the case of the house, as well as for repairs to the house. So, honestly consider if you have to know how to do any of these things for a property. If you currently don't know how to do these things, do you have the means to learn how to do them? Think simply; general maintenance, repairs and 'touch up' painting. Electrical and plumbing work will not be included, unless you are certified to do this work. Certification is necessary for these qualified tasks, for both insurance purposes and human safety, too.

Do You Know People Who Can Help You?

So, actually knowing someone who is a contractor or has experience in a trade, is going to save you loads of time. Instead of having to build up a trusted relationship with the people you are going to be working with, you will already be sure that things are running smoothly. This is with respect to the home you are currently renting out, for contracted services that are rendered. Always, always make sure that the contractors are certified to do the work they have been hired to do. For insurance purposes, safety and satisfaction. Trusted contractors are a great asset to you, as a successful property investor/manager.

Can You Handle a Twenty-Four Hour Commitment?

So, whilst you are going to have the option to hire a property management company, this is an expense that will cut into your profits. If you are going to forgo the possibility of a property manager, you will actually need to be prepared to handle calls coming in from your tenants, at all hours of the day. This is especially true in cases of emergency, (for plumbing, water, sewerage or electrical issues). Unfortunately, they happen at odd hours sometimes. You need to be able to cope with sudden changes that may occur unexpectedly.

Do You Like to Deal with People?

Did you know that when you choose tenants - you are actually choosing people you are going to be relying upon? Fundamentally, they will actually be entrusted to take care of *your house,* and pay their rent, on time; over and over again. You may not always be able to choose people that you like, and occasionally personalities may even clash. You need to have the skills to work with individuals; who may have different personalities and values to you. You also need to be able to work with complete strangers, for contracting or service needs as required.

Do You Have the Finances to Purchase the Properties?

When you are buying a home with a mortgage you are going to need to have approval for the credit, as well as the funding for the down payment. Even if you do have those things, there is one other thing to consider. Since there are often situations where you may find yourself without a tenant, you need to make sure that you are going to be able to pay the mortgage and expenses, (for the time you are without a tenant).

Being a landlord is different than being a private homeowner. It is primarily a functioning business, and it needs to be treated like one, for success and future profitability. Ensure that you take the time to really plan what you are going to do before you jump in. Because the last thing you want, is to go in without a plan and find yourself on the other side of the transaction - with less money and no property.

If, after reading this chapter, you are still sure that you are ready to embark on the journey into the investment property market, read on. Then you can start to find out how to select a rental property, as well as a great neighborhood to buy into, as well. And, more importantly, we are also going to go over the steps that you are going to have to take, in order to obtain that great investment property. Then you may begin renting it out to an individual or a family unit.

Chapter 3: Choosing A Rental Property

Aright, so when it comes to choosing the rental property you are going to invest in, there are many different things you need to take into consideration. The first thing you need to decide, is what kind of property you are going to invest in.

Typically speaking, a single family dwelling is a good choice for beginners who are embarking upon the property investment world. However, it is also a really good idea to consider all of your options. This includes all of the pros and cons of each choice; undertaken before making your final decision.

Commercial Real Estate Investments

These investments consist of things like office buildings, for example. You can get a small building with individual rooms. These can be leased out to small business owners and/or companies; who would pay you to use the property. Typically speaking, these types of agreements include terms of more than one year, which leads to more financial stability. However, you must be aware that with the conditions being locked in for a longer time, you could miss out on the opportunity to make more money. This is especially true if the rental margin rates were to increase substantially - over a short period of time.

Industrial Real Estate Investments

This type of investment could consist of anything (from industrial warehouses to distribution centers to storage units and other special purposes of real estate). These types of investments typically have a higher startup fee. They are still great to consider for your investment portfolio, nonetheless.

Retail Real Estate Investments

This type of investment could beneficially include: shopping malls, strip malls, and stand along retail storefronts. These usually take a lot more work to upkeep, and may include parking lots, as well as other specialty services to the tenants.

Residential Real Estate Investments

For the sake of this book, we are going to get into the most depth in this category, exponentially. These types of properties include: houses, townhouses, buildings, and vacation homes. All of which we are going to look at more in more thorough detail.

Single Family Rental Properties

These are properties that only have one family in them. You pay the mortgage and the property taxes, and then the tenants pay you a monthly fee to inhabit the home. In most cases, the tenant is responsible for the core upkeep of the house; yard work, etc., as well as paying for the monthly bills, as well. Although sometimes this is not always the case. This type of property usually attracts longer term renters. Normally the people who are looking for this kind of property are financially stable, because they are a part of a family (or a couple), who is looking to begin a family in the future.

There are many advantages to starting with a small, single dwelling house. This is going to give you the chance to see if the property investment business really suits you. And starting with just a single home will allow you to get an idea of the maintenance; bookkeeping, and other processes involved in becoming an investment property owner/manager.

Condos

Condos are very appealing properties, because you don't need to worry about many of the external repairs. Many of the external concerns are handled by the Condo Association. However, you are typically going to get a lower rent for a condo as you will also need to pay condo fees on top of your other expenditure. Sometimes a higher rent may be charged, because of the modernized amicability and ambience. Location and condition will factor in, with regard to the price achievable, for various condos.

Student Rental Properties

These are properties that you would purchase in the vicinity of, or nearby to a university or college. Most often these rentals have students that rent them, from September until May. You can usually get a higher rent for them too, since the lease is shorter than the standard one year. Another bonus to this type of rental is that you can also set a house up, in a style similar to a dorm. Then it can be rented out to various students - who would also increase your property investment income. On the other hand, this type of rental is going to require you to be a lot more 'hands-on,' as you are more likely going to have some repairs to do by the end of the lease. This may not always be true, but it is worth considering.

Duplexes and Triplexes

Renting a duplex or a triplex is similar to renting out two single, family dwellings, except both families are on the same property. Each of the two or three tenants would have their own gas and water meters, though. One major advantage to this over a single family dwelling, is that if one of your tenants moves out, the other tenant is able to offset the costs associated with having an empty suite. These can be great money spinners in the right location.

Apartment Buildings

Taking on an apartment building may seem overwhelming, but one advantage is that you can get income from multiple tenants, and only have the upkeep of one building. Similar to a duplex, if you suddenly have tenants move out, you are going to have others who are able to offset your costs, exponentially. One disadvantage of an apartment building, however, is that you are now having to oversee many different tenants - which means you could be dealing with a lot more repairs, as well.

Vacation Houses

Investing in vacation homes is not recommended for those who are new to the property investment market. This is because you are going to have a constant turnover of people who are staying in the home, and you are going to need to provide a furnished home. One which is going to mean that you are open to incurring more damages. Another disadvantage is that unless you live in an area that is considered to be a vacation destination, it is going to be hard to check into the property. Especially after a tenant leaves, which forces you into hiring someone to manage and/or maintain it for you.

Now that you have a good understanding of all of the investment properties that are available to you, you are ready to select the one that you think is going to best suit your strengths. You can write a pros and cons list for your favorites, if you like. That will help your decision making process a lot.

Once you have decided which type of property you are going to invest in, it's time to consider the demographic that you want to rent to, and also choose the locality or area that you want to invest in.

Chapter 4: Consider The Area That You Want to Invest In

When it comes to choosing the location of the property you want to invest in, there are many things you will want to consider. Here, we are going to look at the top things you need to take into consideration.

Amenities

Look into the neighborhoods you are considering, including: parks, malls, movie theaters, public transportation, and other amicable or fundamental positives. You can see what the neighborhood has currently, as well as what amenities are going to be added in the near foreseeable future.

Crimes

No one wants to live in the middle of a criminal activity hot spot. Look into the statistics for crime in the area that you are considering. Additionally, you can look into the vandalism rates, petty crimes, and serious crime offences, too. Check into whether the crime rates are increasing or decreasing. You can also ask about the police presence in the neighborhood. Remember, location is important for the future success of your investment business property.

Demographics

When you are looking into neighborhoods, it is important for you to consider the demographic characteristics that you are hoping to rent to. If you are looking to rent to university students; you should keep your potential neighborhoods limited to those located nearby, or around universities.

Job Market

Areas that feature growing employment opportunities, are often more attractive to people who are looking to rent a home. Where there are employment opportunities, there are people who are looking for somewhere close to work, and to live. This is a fundamental element of *all* property investment.

Listing and Vacancies

Pay attention to how many listings there are for the area that you are considering buying in. If there is an unusually high number for one neighborhood, this can be a signal of an area that has a negative element or elements. And it could be a seasonal cycle. It is also important to consider how many vacancies there are in the area. If there is a high number of vacancies, you are likely going to be forced to lower your rent in order to find tenants, whereas if there is a lower number of vacancies; you are more likely going to be able to increase your rent.

Property Taxes

Property taxes are not stable across the board, and change from neighborhood to neighborhood. This is definitely something you are going to want to take into consideration. So, when you have decided where to purchase your rental property, then that will be a cost that is going to have to be factored into the rate. Factored into that amount you are going to be charging for your rental.

Rent Rates

Since the rent you are charging is going to be how you are earning your income; it is important to know what the average rent in the area you are looking at is. If the average rent is not going to be enough to cover your mortgage and property taxes, you should probably keep looking.

Schools

When you are renting out a single family dwelling, you are likely going to be renting to a family who has a child in school. Knowing the reputation of the school that is in the area, you are considering purchasing in can help you determine if it is a good value. While the main concern right now is going to be your monthly cash flow, in the long run, the overall value of the home is going to matter when it comes time to sell the home.

Other Things to Keep in Mind

A couple of other things to look into is how the area is expected to develop in the near future, as well as things that might affect your insurance.

If there is a lot of new condos and malls, then you are probably getting into a good growth area. However, it is important to keep an eye out for growth that could 'hurt' your rental property, such as a noisy, smoky factory or the removal of play equipment or green spaces.

When it comes to considering your insurance rates, you are going to want to know if the area you are looking at is prone to flooding or earthquakes. Paying for the extra insurance you may need for these occurrences, can really eat away at your potential income.

When you are looking for your ideal rental property, remember that it is going to take some footwork, to find a good property in a good neighborhood. It needs to appeal to renters, so they can afford it, and also enjoy it, as much as possible.

Keeping the property that you are considering buying in an area you know, is a good way to make sure that you are going to have a successful rental investment. When you purchase in an area you don't know (just because the price seems irresistible), you might run into problems that you weren't necessarily anticipating.

Chapter 5: Things You Need to Know About Financing an Investment Property

If you have decided that you are ready to look for financing, there are a few things that you need to know about financing before you head out to the bank. Being thoroughly prepared, can help you make sure that you have everything in place. That way, you are more likely to find a lender to give you the money, for the house you want to purchase.

You Are Going to Need a Down Payment

If you are buying a rental home that you aren't going to be living in, you are going to need at least twenty percent. This figure is for the cost of the home; as a down payment. If you are purchasing 2-4 units you only need to place 3.5% down if you will be owner-occupying one of the units. But, if you are not occupying any of the units you will need to place 20% down. So, really consider how much the home you are looking at purchasing is going to cost, and make sure that you are going to have the required down payment... before you head out excitedly to the bank.

You Want to Be a Strong Borrower

The biggest influence on whether or not you are going to be granted a loan is going to be your *credit score*. If you have a lower credit score, you are more likely going to have to pay a higher interest rate, and in some cases, you may be denied a loan altogether. So focus on your credit score in every transaction or financial purchase. This is indeed a great asset to property investment, so keep it well rated, at all costs.

Choose The Right Lender

While it might seem like a good idea just to go into your traditional bank and ask for the mortgage, this isn't always the case. In many scenarios, choosing a small community bank is the better option. The reason a small community bank could be a better option, is because they usually have more flexibility, and they also like to be able to invest back into their communities, too. The other option that is worth looking into - is a mortgage broker. A mortgage broker is able to access more mortgage products, and can usually find you a better rate than banks are able to. Ensuring that you are going to choose the right lender; right from the beginning, is the best way to ensure you are getting the best rates.

Going with A Mortgage Broker

If you have decided to go with a mortgage broker, there are a few things you are going to want to take into consideration. First, if you are looking for the best rates, as well as flexibility, no-fee brokers with professional experience are the way to go. If you aren't sure how to gauge their experience, ask how many properties they have financed in the last year. If the number is less than ten to fifteen, you are probably going to want to select someone with more long term experience.

Know Your Total Debt Ratio

In order to be approved for a mortgage, your total debt ratio must fall within your lender's limits. To put it simply, your total debt ratio is your total monthly expenses divided by your total monthly income from all sources, of income. As simple as this sounds, it's really not. Some lenders aren't going to recognize one hundred percent of your rental income, which is going to make it harder for you to qualify for a mortgage. Just scout for the best deal, and remember that mortgage brokers have a wealth of knowledge to 'tap' into.

Know The Features to Look for

When you are getting a mortgage for a property that you are planning on renting out, there are certain things that you are going to want to look for in a great lender. Going for a more flexible lender is going to mean that you might have higher rates. However, this is often worth it. There are a few of the things you are going to want to ask about when it comes to prospective lenders. Read on for more information on these, now.

Flexible Rental Income Rules

As we briefly covered previously, some lenders are going to allow you to claim one hundred percent of your total rental amount within your income, and some are only going to allow you to claim fifty percent. So, the more you can claim - the better the flexibility (and higher loan achievability). So search for the best lenders. This is your financial investment. You have the ultimate say in what you want, for your future and income leverage.

Allows A Higher Debt Ratio

Some lenders only allow you to have a forty percent total debt ratio, while others will allow you to have forty-two percent. The two percent may not seem like a big deal, but it is; especially when you begin owning more than just one or two rental properties.

Allows Property to Be in A Company Name

Putting the property into a company name (instead of your personal name), is going to give you more liability protection, than if you were to buy all of your properties under your own name.

Allows You to Finance Multiple Properties

Whilst it isn't an official rule, many banks will not finance you for more than three or four properties. So, if you are hoping to build an empire, you are going to want to select a lender that has experience working with people who own many properties. Another plus to this, is that a lender who is accustomed to working with people (with more properties), is also more likely to allow you to count all of your rental income. So that it will be accounted for; into your total debt ratio.

Allows Longer Amortization

A longer amortization is going to allow you to optimize your cash flow, and ensure that you are able to do the repairs and such, as they are needed. You are usually able to place extra money on your mortgage (if you have the finances available to do so).

Allows A Second Mortgage

Taking a second mortgage on a house that you are renting, can actually give you the down payment that you need, in order to purchase a second rental property. If you aren't able to take a second mortgage on your rental property, you are going to need to save up for the second down payment, however.

Will Lend On Large Mortgages

Some lenders aren't willing to lend on large mortgages; the downfall to this is that you are going to be limited in your options, fundamentally. You may not be able to purchase in one of the better neighborhoods that you were hoping to gain rent in. Ask a mortgage broker for advice on this. They will give this information freely, and it is vitally important to your cause. Great information is always a plus, in the world of property investment. Get as much advice as you can.

Offers A Line of Credit

A line of credit with your mortgage is a huge bonus. It will allow you to do any of the work that needs to be done to your new property (usually right away), and will also allow you to have backup money for when you need to do any repairs.

Chapter 6: Purchasing Your Property – The Real Estate Agent

Now that you have been approved for a mortgage, it is time to head out and find the perfect property. The first thing you are going to do is get in touch with a local real estate agent.

A real estate agent is going to be able to get you a lot more information on properties than you are going to be able to for yourself. For a home buyer, an agent is typically free, in most situations, the agent is paid when you purchase a home, by the seller. However, you don't want to call up the first real estate agent whose ad looks good. Like with anything, you need to do your research and make sure you are selecting a real estate agent who is going to serve you best.

Ask About Their Specialties

You may think that since the real estate agent is helping you to buy a home and not selling your home for you, that their specialty doesn't matter. However, this couldn't be further from the truth. If you are looking for a property that you are going to be renting out, find an agent who is accustomed to working with investors. This will mean that your agent will be able to show you properties that might make good rental investment opportunities.

Look Up Their Licensing

Some states have boards that are responsible for licensing and disciplining the real estate agents within that state. Check to ensure that the person you are going to be working with is licensed, and if there have been any complaints or disciplinary actions taken against the real estate agent. You need to work with a professional, qualified professional.

Awards Matter

Look for 'decorated' agents. They have worked extremely hard to earn their awards. An award that really means something is, *Realtor of the Year*. This designation is usually given by their peers in the industry, and means that they are being endorsed by other agents; not just by their statistics.

Look in to Their Credentials

The letters that come after a real estate agent's name are very important. Each acronym shows that the agent has taken additional courses in order to become more well-versed, in specific areas of real estate sales. This can be anything from *CRS* (Certified Residential Specialist) to *ABR* (Accredited Buyer's Representative).

Find Out How Long They Have Been in Business

Choosing an agent who has only been in business for a few years, means that they are usually still going to be learning while helping you buy a property. Selecting someone who practices full time and has been for many years, is important. Then you know that you are going to have an agent who is more likely to be well versed, knowledgeable and engaged in what they are doing. Remember, you are buying a large investment to create an income. A great agent is very important to you, now.

Check Out Their Current Listings

There are a few different things you need to look here. These factors are important when perusing the current listings of a prospective real estate agent. And one of the first things you want to know is - that they have enough listings that show they are active in what they do. You also want to ensure that the listings that the agent has on file, are similar to the ones you are looking for. This will help to ensure that the agent is familiar with working in a familiar price range ratio, as well as understanding the type of house or property that you are looking to buy.

Ask About Other Properties in The Area

A real estate agent who is good at what they do, is going to know about other properties that are available, (usually off the top of their head). You want an agent who is on top of the market, and 'switched on.' This is because they are more likely to be watching for new properties that come onto the market. Then they can let you know when something comes up - that matches what you are looking for. Your agent can be a great asset to you. So, try and build a relationship, early on. Good agents have a wealth of knowledge to share with you.

So, additionally, keep in mind how well the real estate agent listens, when you tell them what you are looking for. If the agent you have selected is showing you houses that don't match your criteria, it might be time to find a different agent. Most agents will want to help you succeed, though. Just be aware that their knowledge and expertise are paramount to your future success. You are discerning for professional, financial reasons. Don't be afraid to look around. It is your decision, and your investment.

Chapter 7: Purchasing Your Property – The Offer

Once you have found the property that you want to purchase and you have *physically* walked through it, then forward movement can occur. When you have decided that it is going to meet your needs, and gained a property building report, the next thing you need to do is make a monetary offer on the property. A property building report is always recommended to check for structural defects, white ants, salt damp etc.

Also, there is more to consider about the house than just the amount of money you are going to pay for the house, which in itself is a very important factor. In this chapter, we are going to look at all of the things you need to take into consideration when you are making an offer on an investment property.

Firstly, it is important to know that there are two different types of offers you can make on a home. You can make a *firm offer* or a *conditional offer*.

Firm Offer

This is the type of offer that a seller wants to see. It means that you want to purchase the house without there being any conditions to be met. So, no clauses that are "subject to," anything.

Conditional Offer

This is an offer that is contingent on the "subject to" factors being met. The sale could be subject to a home inspection, financing approval, or even to the sale of the buyer's existing home. Remember, that the sale isn't final until all of the conditions have been met.

The factors that you are going to want to keep in mind when it comes to making an offer on a home include the: price, deposit, terms, inclusions, exclusions and the closing day for making an offer.

Price

Make sure that you are keeping your emotions out of your purchase. While you don't want to make an offer that is too low, keep in mind that you also don't want to make an offer that is higher than what you are willing to spend, either. At the end of the day, you are doing this to make money, and you need to be prepared to walk away from a purchase if it isn't going the way you want it to. This is *just* a financial transaction, so put your emotional ego away!

Deposit

Putting a deposit on the house is considered to be an act of good faith, and shows that you are serious about the purchase of the property. The deposit that you put on the house will be applied to the final price of the house when the sale closes. The seller of a property will take your offer more seriously too, if there is a firm deposit.

Inclusions and Exclusions

Your offer might be contingent on the seller's willingness to include or exclude things from the home. This can apply to appliances, window coverings, decorative items and so on.

Once all of the negotiations have been completed, and you and the seller have agreed to the terms, through the agent, then finalization starts. Then your real estate agent is going to complete a copy of the agreement - showing the sale and purchase with the final terms. Once this is done, the agreement should be reviewed by a real estate lawyer, to ensure that the terms are exactly as you want them, legally.

Once you have completed this process and everything is signed, all you need to do is wait for the closing date to come around; so you can officially enter your property.

Chapter 8: Getting Ready to Find a Renter

Preparing a property for rental

Now that you own the property you are going to be using for rental income, the next step is to get it ready for a tenant/renter. Also, congratulations for making it this far, (if you have already purchased a property).

Depending on the condition of the house when you bought it, you might have some work that you need to do before you can list it for rent. While you don't want to overdo the number of improvements that can be done, there are a few requirements that you want the property to meet. Let's call them standards, for our purposes.

Getting your property up to sufficient standard for a tenant to live in, can be a little daunting. Things that you might not normally find essential or important, can actually make a massive difference. We want somebody to be excited to rent your home or apartment.

Creating a safety checklist should be your number one priority; ensuring all smoke alarms, locks and doors are secure. This should be fairly straight forward. Fit your smoke alarm with brand new batteries and test them out prior to any inspections. Going through your property and testing all the windows and doors should be next on your list. And does that sliding window in the master bedroom have a key to unlock it? Double check! How about the jammed door handle? Can you fix that yourself or do you need to call someone? These small things all add up. Once you've thoroughly sorted out any potential safety issues, next comes the aesthetics:

- **Any maintenance work.** Do any walls need patching up or painting? How about that missing door knob in the kitchen!
- **General garden tidy up.** Even if your property just has a balcony, are there any dead plants or pots that need to be cleared? If you have a large garden and there is some substantial work to be done, you should consider hiring a landscape team to do a tidy up before even taking photographs of the property.

- **Pest control.** Even if you don't think there are any unsuspected critters running through your floorboards, there could be. To be safe and to save yourself trouble later on have a thorough pest inspection, and hire an exterminator to guarantee the property's cleanliness.
- **Appliance upkeep.** Does the property come with a dish washer or washing machine? If so, are they in working order or would it be better to get rid of them, or replace them? Even if it does add a slight amount of value to the property it would be very frustrating and time consuming if there were constant issues with the given appliances.
- **Keys.** This sounds a tad obvious - but how many keys do you have cut for the property? And do you have multiples of all the keys needed on the property, for every window, door and gate? You will need to make one copy for yourself, and at least two for the tenant depending on how many adults are living at the property address.
- **Décor.** Keeping the whole house as cohesive as possible, is always a good idea; eliminating feature walls, over the top artworks and any valuable furniture - means that you can show your property as a blank canvas for your potential tenants. Another helpful hint, is to open up all the windows and doors just before the showing; to allow fresh air and bright light to illuminate your property.

Hygienic and Clean

You want to make sure that the house you are going to be renting out is hygienically clean. Remember, renters aren't likely to take care of the house the way you would. Sometimes less carpeting and more hard flooring options are easier to deal with later; after a tenant's lease has expired and they move out. Make sure the home is always spotless and hygienic. You want to attract renters.

Empty

Make sure that there is nothing being stored in the basement, attic or any of the cupboards. You don't want there to be any dispute about whether something was in the house or not when your tenants move out. Make your life as easy as possible here. Let them have all the space, because they are paying for it. It is also somewhat unprofessional to have your belongings on the property. So, keep it empty for your tenant.

Free from Major Repair

While the house may need updating, you will definitely want to make sure that there aren't any major repairs that are going to need to be done. Major repairs that are waiting to be done - are going to be a turn off to prospective renters. They will also bring down the amount you are able to rent the property for. A home inspection should be done during the buying process, by hiring a home inspector (your realtor can arrange this), to ensure hassle free purchasing. Also, this is a normal part of the process unless the home is sold 'as-is.'

Up to Code

It is imperative that you make sure that the house meets all code requirements. If the electrical, plumbing or any other aspect isn't up to code, it can bring a lot of problems your way in the future. Again, this can be done during the inspection period when purchasing the home. Never rent out a property that does not meet the code standards, because tenants can actually complain. Some may even report the home for unsatisfactory living conditions, if they feel 'put out,' by bad plumbing, faulty electricity or a leaky roof (as examples). Stay ahead of the game, here. It is not fun for the tenant or the landlord, when a home is not up to standard, exponentially. Also, safety is paramount for anyone living in a rental home. The elderly and even children can be affected. So, don't leave anything to chance, here.

Setting A Price

Before you can list your property as available for rent, you need to know how much you are going to be asking for. In order to do this, you need to know what the market is going to allow you to rent your house for. Luckily, it isn't hard to come across this information, all it takes is a little locality research.

To get an idea of what a fair price is going to be to ask for, consider what other houses in the area are going for. Look at the rent that is being asked for, for houses that are a similar size, condition, and location.

When you are comparing other houses to yours, there are also some additional things you may need to take into consideration.

How Many Bedrooms and Bathrooms Are There?

If you are comparing your three bedrooms and two-bathroom home to another rental property that is a two bedroom and one bathroom, you aren't going to get a good representation of what you should ask for rent. You can still compare, and write a list.

What Utilities Are Included?

Another factor is whether or not you are going to be including utilities. If you have chosen not to include utilities, your rent is going to need to be a little lower than another home of the same size that comes with all of the utilities included.

Is Parking Included?

Parking may be hard to come by in the area you are going to be renting a property in. So, you are going to be able to charge a little extra in rent, if you can provide a private parking spot for your tenant.

Any Additional Benefits?

Some added benefits might include free Wi-Fi, cable or lawn mowing services. All of these can be taken into consideration when you are setting out your rental fee.

Are Pets Allowed?

If you are going to be allowing pets into your property, you are within your rights to ask for a pet rental fee to cover any damages that are caused by the pet. You may charge 'a touch more,' on a weekly or monthly basis too.

Is The Property Furnished?

One of the biggest factors in what you are charging for rent is whether or not you are providing all of the furnishings in the home. If you are, you are going to want to charge more to cover anything that might need to be replaced or repaired when your tenants move out.

Once you have established exactly what your property has to offer, it's time to go out and look at properties that are similar to determine what the fair market value is going to be.

The easiest way to find out what the rents are like in your area is to drive around and call any "for rent" signs you see.

You can also check the rental listings online, and look for properties that are in the same area and offer the same things you are offering, as well.

Check the newspaper or ask members of your local *Landlord's Association*.

Once you have built up a large enough sample of the properties, you can average out the data and use that as the fair market rate. Add them all up, then divide by the number of properties you have added. So, as an example: ten properties...add the rent's up (monthly), and then divide by 10, to get your average monthly figure.

Security Deposits

On top of the rent, renters are required to give a security deposit. Keep in mind; this is a deposit and not a fee. Since it is not a fee, it is strongly recommended that you keep this money in a separate bank account to be returned to the tenant when they move out, less any damages that you need to repair because of them. Check into local legislation regarding what you should charge for a deposit. Some states have no limits, while others do. Typically, landlords charge the equivalent of one month's rent, unless the prospective tenants have anything worrisome in their background, in which case you can request more.

Advertising Your Property

Once you have worked out all of the details about your property, you are ready to reach out to prospective tenants. When you are looking to attract tenants to your property, you want to reach as many tenants as possible - and as fast as you can. There are three main ways that you can advertise about a property rental.

Newspaper

This is one of the most expensive ways of advertising, but it is able to reach a lot of people. When you post in the newspaper, you are forced to keep to the minimum amount of information - and that means that people need to call you to find out the details of the property you are renting. This is a good thing, because you can start screening them, over the phone, to suit you.

Yard Signs

This is one of the oldest ways to advertise your property to potential tenants. There are two setbacks to this method, however. One is that you are relying on people to drive past your property. The second, is that it is an instant notification that the house is empty. Sometimes being empty can attract negativity, because locals may ask why. Why has no-one rented that home…what is wrong with it? Of course there may be nothing wrong with it at all, but people will always make judgements about things; it is human nature. So, be aware of this factor.

Online

This is quickly becoming one of the most popular ways to share a rental property. You can include pictures and as much information as you would like about the property. This instantly filters through the people who are contacting you and limits it to people who are genuinely interested in the property.

When you are creating your ads, (especially to be posted online), you want to make sure that you include all of the pertinent information. You don't want to have to screen through three hundred calls a day all from people who are asking what the amount of the rent is.

You also want to ensure that you are emphasizing the features that your property provides, and that make it a better option than the other houses on the market. You also want to mention a little bit about the neighborhood, such as being nearby to schools or public transits. The more you are able to share about a rental property, the more the prospective renter is able to see themselves living there.

Another great idea, is to include pictures that clearly show the potential that the property has. A few pictures that show the size of the rooms as well as the condition they are in, is usually enough to attract people who are genuinely interested in renting the property.

Remember, to be honest in what you are posting. There is nothing to be gained by being misleading in your ads. It is also unprofessional. State the price and the conditions of the lease as clearly as you can. If a potential tenant realizes that you were misleading, they aren't going to want to rent from you - and are probably going to tell others to avoid you as well. Always be honest, professional and open with people. This is a great way to do successful business.

Be sure to include both an email address and a phone number and do your best to be available to answer all emails and phone calls. Many people who are looking for a home to rent, are likely to be calling more landlords (than just you). So, if you are available, you are more likely to be able to 'scoop them up,' before they move along to something else.

Chapter 9: Selecting A Renter

Now that you have posted your ad, the next step is to sit back and wait for potential tenants to reach out to you.

Prescreening Potential Renters

When you receive a phone call from a prospective renter, it is helpful if you are able to prescreen them over the phone. This will save you some time showing the property to people who aren't in a position to afford the rent. The rental criteria you set is ultimately up to you, but the list below shows some standard criteria that landlords look for in a tenant.

As a necessity, the gross monthly income needs to be approximately three times (or more), than the monthly rent amount. This is to ensure that the tenant is going to be able to pay the rent successfully each month.

Applicants must have a favorable credit history, or at least a favorable renting history. If an applicant hasn't been paying a credit card but has paid his rent on time for the last ten years, he is probably a 'safe bet' to rent to.

Applicants must be employed, or earning an income from another source, and be able to show a proof of income, as well.

The number of occupants must be within the limits that are set out by state laws. Some states have a limit of two occupants per bedroom. Check the details for your locality or area.

Reading this list over the phone and asking the prospective client if they meet these qualifications, makes it easier to turn them down if they do not meet them. It helps to take the emotion out of renting to someone, so it is a good idea to prescreen. Imperative, actually. You are relying on them to pay, on time, every time.

Allowing a tenant to rent from you who doesn't meet your minimum qualifications, is going to set you up for failure later on. However, you do need to be sure that the questions you are asking are worded in a way that they aren't discriminatory. You cannot ask a person their personal information such as: race, skin color, gender, national origin, religion, disability, or family status. Be professional and non-judgmental, always.

<u>Communicating with a Potential Tenant</u>

Taking enquiries will be one of the first opportunities you get to really meet and get to know a potential tenant. Whilst obviously being in person gives you a much better grasp of the tenant as a person, you can also gain a pretty strong understanding from the initial phone call. Certain factors to take into consideration include:

- Asking pushy questions for example: How many people have already applied?
- Is the rent negotiable?
- Are they rushing you off the phone?
- Do they sound genuine and sincere in their interest?
- Are they polite?

Always remember that you are potentially going to have to deal with this person on a regular basis; anywhere from six months to two years, so take your time in deciding.

If you do decide to show your property to them and they then choose to send in an application, there are certain questions that you will definitely need to include on the forms. Always ask appropriate questions. Here are some, but are not limited to:

- What is your reason for moving?
- Are you currently employed?
- What is your monthly income?
- Do you have any online profiles?
- Will you have a security deposit and one month's rent upon moving in?
- Do you have any pets? If so what are they?
- How would you describe your lifestyle?
- Do you have any rental references?
- Do you have any questions for me?

By asking these questions (and hopefully by the potential tenant answering them honestly), you will be able to garner not only their personality, but their ability to live up to your standards. E.g. Keeping a tidy property, and paying the rent on time; without question.

Of course some things are completely out of your control (that you can't ever predict happening. So, a simple way to make sure the tenant you pick isn't going to be difficult - is by only choosing tenants with a solid rental history. It might seem like there are a ton of young couples and singles out there looking for a place to rent, but without a rental background it can be hard to judge whether or not they will be a good tenant. If, however, you pick someone with a rental guarantor or reference; you will be able to call that person up and ask them questions about your potential tenant. A few questions you should definitely ask any rental reference:

- Were there any incidents of violent or anti-social behavior?
- Did they pay their rent on time?
- Did they house any unapproved animals or people whilst living there?
- What type of condition did they leave the house in?

When it comes to choosing a tenant whether you're self-managing the property or hiring a property manager, is unimportant really. Because being involved in the screening process for picking a tenant will not only give you peace of mind, but it will also let you form a relationship with the tenant. Be clear and concise with what you will and will not accept, for example: no people with a criminal history, must be employed, no more than X number of people etc. Be clear before you screen them. This is paramount.

By setting out your limits and expectations clearly, there won't be too much wiggle room for tenants. However, always keep an open mind and be willing to meet the tenant for inspections and signings, *before* making a final decision. Remember, reading about a person on an application is very different from having a face to face conversation (it gives them less of a chance to lie).

Showing The Property

Once you have prescreened the potential tenants, the next step is to show them the property. Unfortunately, a lot of the time, people aren't going to show up when they say they are going to. There are two different ways you can approach this.

1. Give them the address of the property and have them drive past the house. If they are still interested, they can then call you back and then set up an appointment to see the inside. Additionally, this eliminates the people who aren't interested once they see the area.

2. Batch your showings together. This means that you tell all prospective tenants that you are going to be at the house during a specific time and tell them that they can come by then - to see the property. This ensures that someone is likely to come to look at the property. While it can be a little awkward to have multiple people checking out a property at the same time, it also creates a sense of competition and scarcity which tends to result in more applications.

When people come to view the property, be sure to include a copy of the criteria and the application process; with the application, so that prospective tenants know what the process is going to be.

The Application Process

It is important to give every person who is interested in your property an application, even if you aren't interested in renting to them. Again, this is to protect you from being charged or accused of discrimination. It is a good idea to encourage tenants to fill out the application right there. However, some people are going to want to take it home with them, and bring it back to you at a later time. So, you may need to be prepared to deal with this occurrence, as well.

The Rental Application

When you are creating your application, you are going to want to make sure that you are asking for all of the information. So, you are going to need to get a clear picture as to whether they are going to make a good, reliable tenant. An ideal application should include:

- Names of all potential adult renters.
- Date of birth.
- Social Security numbers.
- Phone number/s.
- Alternate phone number/s.
- Previous addresses (including the last two to five years).
- Current employer (name, hire date, income, contact information).

- Previous employer (name, dates worked, contact information).
- Emergency contact/s.
- Release of information statement.
- Signature of all tenants applying.

Application Fee

An application fee is definitely advisable. Check with your state laws and make sure that you are allowed to charge a fee, and make sure that you aren't charging more than you are allowed to, as well. An application fee will cover the cost of the background check, as well as for your time to check through all of their specific information. If tenants are serious about wanting to rent, they aren't going to have a problem with paying the fee. So be aware of that.

Immediate Disqualifications

When you get an application and fee from a tenant, be sure to look it over to ensure that it meets your criteria. If it doesn't meet the criteria that you have set out for a tenant, it should be immediately disqualified without you wasting your time on a background check. This is a business, and you must stay grounded and professional, always.

Background and Credit Checks

When you run your background and credit checks, it is up to your discretion what is going to make or break a tenant's chances. If you have a large pool of applications, then you can be picky and choose the one that has the highest qualifications. However, if you are struggling to find someone to take the rental, you may need to loosen your standards a little bit, to find someone who is suitable. Again, this doesn't mean you should let just anyone rent your property, but enables you to place more emphasis on the things that are most important to you. You are the boss, here. So be discerning for the success of your business.

Verifying Income and Rental History

We want to believe that the people who are applying to live in our properties are honest, but that often isn't always the case. The release of information statement that they filled out is going to allow you to call the people that the applicant indicated, on their application. Once you have checked out everything - you are ready to let the applicant know.

It is important to process all of your applications on a first come, first served basis. When you have denied an applicant, it is important to inform them with a letter that clearly states why they have been declined. When you find an applicant who has been approved, you can let them know verbally. Remember to treat people kindly and professionally.

Holding The Property

Once you have let a tenant know that they have been approved to rent a property, it is important to let them know that you require a deposit to hold the property. Most landlords require that this is given to them within twenty-four hours. However, you can use your discretion, here.

A Good Relationship with Tenants

You might think it is all up to the tenant to behave accordingly, whilst residing in your property. But, it's also up to you as the landlord and owner to manage expectations and act professionally. If you want to keep good tenants, be a good landlord. Don't let little things slip your mind. Whether it's a small tap leak your tenant called you about five times (and you still haven't gotten around to calling a plumber). Alternatively, if there are issues with the neighbors that need your help to be resolved, it's up to you to help the rental tenancy run smoothly. Be available and professional, at all times.

Collecting rent can be a little bit uncomfortable and there are certain customs and expectations put on both the landlord and tenant, here. So, if you're managing the property yourself, there are three factors you need to make sure you always keep in mind:

- **Never 'pop in' to collect rent money.** Set a date, whether it be the beginning, middle or end of the month and stick to those dates. If possible, set up a direct bank transfer with the tenant so there are no confusions or delays. Never go over to collect rent money in cash.
- **Do not accept partial payments.** Not even once! By doing this you will make your tenant feel as though they have some sort of control over you. If they absolutely need to do a partial payment, make sure it happens once and only once!
- **Communicate with the same person.** If there is only one tenant that makes it pretty simple but if there are multiple

people living in your rental property - try to ensure you mainly communicate with one person most of the time. This makes sure every previous agreement or conversation won't have to be repeated or forgotten.
- ***Keep track of their utilities.*** Whether the utilities are under the tenant's name or yours, sometimes landlords are unaware that their tenants have been avoiding paying the utility bills like water, gas and electricity. To have peace of mind you could have the bills addressed to yourself, or simply charge the tenant's an additional fee on top of the rent to cover the utilities. Either way it's always good to have a handle on the utilities, especially when they move out and you realize they haven't been paying! Setting up a contract with utility inclusions is strongly advised.

Inspections

Once you've found a tenant and everything is (hopefully) going swimmingly there are some matters that still need to be dealt with on a regular basis. This includes inspections, property valuations and dealing with any potential issues. Inspections are a great way to understand how the tenant is not only treating your property but it also allows you to take into consideration if you need to start the process of finding a new tenant.

Organizing an inspection should be fairly straight forward, try to organize a time that suits the tenant, by being considerate during this process they're a lot more likely to be cooperative with the whole inspection. So, if your tenant works nights and doesn't wake up until midday; perhaps setting up an inspection at 9am wouldn't go down so well. Keep an open line of communication, and work around schedules to make it happen. Some things to look out for during an inspection include:

- Any noticeable damage.
- The amount of rubbish or build-up of furniture.
- Checking all door handles for damage.
- Stains/damage to the carpet or floorboards.
- Any evidence of an animal or extra person living there.
- If they have made any alterations to the property e.g. painting the walls.

- Ask them if they are having any problems with anything like the shower head not working or locks being broken etc.

Regular inspections not only mean that the tenant probably won't have the chance to damage the property in any way, but if you also have them semi-regularly from the start of their lease; they will be used to it. If you suspect something is going on, order an inspection for the following weekend. Other than that, two or three times in one year is considered acceptable. Monthly is more definite, though.

<u>Maintenance work on the property</u>

If you are fortunate enough to own a property with a pool, tennis court or Jacuzzi, of course that is going to add some much needed value to your home. However, once you have decided to put your property up for lease, deciding whether to charge a maintenance or service fee on top of the rent is a challenge. There are a few ways to figure out which way is going to work best for you and your tenant:

- **Include maintenance fees in the rental price.** This is probably the safest way to go about maintenance and money; including it in the advertised rental price. It might make your property look a tad more expensive, but it ensures the tenant won't be surprised by any unexpected maintenance costs either; when they're signing the lease, or during their stay.
- **Dividing up the maintenance cost.** Somewhere in the rental agreement ensure there is a section where it explains: that half or a quarter (whatever you deem reasonable) of the maintenance expenses will be up to the tenant to pay. Make sure to explain where the costs are going, how much it is, and be sure to give them contact details of the maintenance team you are hiring. So that they can call them up, if they need reassurance on price.
- **Paying for it as it comes.** If you only have your pool serviced once a month, perhaps you would prefer to pay the bill as it comes. Then you can decide whether or not to charge the tenant as it happens. This might seem like the easiest option but it is also the one that has the potential to cause you more stress long term. Probably better to build the price into the rent. Hidden costs for tenants are not advised.

Another issue that landlords face with long time tenants, is how and when to increase the rent. In a competitive real estate market, offering low rent guarantees interest in your property. But what about when other properties like yours are requesting a substantial amount more than you are. As a way to keep tenants happy, it's probably not a good idea to increase the rent until after the first year, or when renewing the rental agreement occurs.

Doing adequate research on similar properties in the area, and finding out what they are charging as well, is a great idea. If you find that you have to increase the rent - approach the situation calmly and rationally.

Show the tenants the research - showing what other properties are going for, and give them enough time to adjust. Don't increase their allotment of rent abruptly; give them ample time to sort out their finances. If, however, they decide that they simply cannot afford the extra rent, it could be time for you to start looking for a new tenant. A few months prior to when the lease is set to expire.

Dealing with difficult tenants

Ideally the tenant you pick will be: immaculate, extremely hygienic and trustworthy. Although that may seem a bit unrealistic - if you do find yourself dealing with somewhat of a difficult tenant, there are certain ways of handling every situation thrown at you as a landlord. Some of the main issues you could potentially have to deal with:

- **Late rent.** This will probably be the most likely issue you will deal with. Although it is obvious that every tenant will have to pay their rent, some like to push the boundaries and see if you'll notice. It's important to remain calm in these situations even if you're very upset; if you don't feel you can calmly respond to them, wait until you are. Once your tenant has explained why the rent is late, hopefully it is a problem that can be resolved easily, e.g. their pay hasn't gone in yet, but they will be able to pay it within 48 hours. As a landlord, give them as many options to pay as possible, so offer to take a check, bank transfer from a different account, and if absolutely necessary – a partial payment. Although, this is not highly recommended.

- ***Unapproved pets.*** First of all, if you want your property to be completely pet free; make sure it is clearly written out in the rental agreement. Then there is not even a chance that they will misunderstand you. Then, if you discover through an inspection that they are keeping pets, you need to take action. If the animals have in some way damaged the property, make it clear that they will be paying for all damages, either with their security deposit or personally. After that, give them a reasonable amount of time to vacate the animals on the grounds. Try to be as understanding as possible - and allow a week or so for the animals to be rehomed. Make sure once this dispute is over with, to regularly check for any further evidence that the animals are still living there, too. Breaching the contract is grounds for termination of the lease agreement.
- ***Violent/Anti-social behavior.*** This is something you will (hopefully) never have to deal with. Whether they have been violent towards you as the landlord or a neighbor or even one another. Then it is a matter that should always be taken seriously. If you find the tenant is becoming aggressive with you either through phone calls, text messages, emails or in person - immediately take note of everything they have said. Next, consult a lawyer if you feel the issue cannot be resolved between you two. Find out your options, and if necessary contact your local police.
- ***Problems with neighbor/s.*** This is a common issue, especially in apartments or condos. As the landlord, it is your duty to resolve the dispute, but it is definitely in your best interests to help the two parties reach an agreement. Speak to your tenant and try to find out what the main issue is, next talk to the neighbor they are having problems with, and find out their side of the story. Acting as a sort of mediator in the situation could help resolve it faster. If, however, there are threats being made or any type of violent behavior, it is best to call the police and let them give the two parties a stern warning. Never place yourself or others, in immediate danger.
- ***Drugs or alcohol abuse.*** This type of problem should always be handled with the utmost care and understanding. If you discover your tenant is consuming illegal substances on your property, and you wish to do something about it, it is entirely up to you. Consult your local law enforcement and/or lawyer. Around one month is more than sufficient, to make sure that there is no damage to the property after you have given your tenant the eviction notice; explain thoroughly to them that you will take anything damaged out of the security deposit. If at a later date they then use you as a rental

reference, make sure to explain the situation you faced with them. Be honest, always.
- ***Breaking the lease.*** If you find yourself in the situation where a tenant intends to break the lease for whatever reason, although it can be a stressful time - it is probably for the best. In terms of compensation, it is fair to charge a fee or the entire rent due until their lease would have ended. If there is a large amount of time until their rent is due, e.g. six months; perhaps charging a fee would be better. It's also a good idea to ask the tenant why they are intending to leave, so you can maybe make those necessary charges for the next tenant, in your rental agreement forms. If you are unsure on how to properly handle the situation at hand, consult a mediator or solicitor to help you find out what has to happen and what your options are. You may also look at the laws specific to your local area.

Chapter 10: Protecting Yourself, Your Property, and Your Tenant

Now that you have the property and a committed tenant, it is time to make sure that the stage is set for you to make money. The first thing you are going to need to do, is to make sure that you have a lease agreement that lays out the expectations and. This includes the incorporations of both the landlord and the tenant. After that is done; you are going to fill out a move-in report, and then start collecting your rent. In this chapter, we are going to look at these things in more depth.

<u>The Rental Lease Agreement</u>

In order to have a legally binding agreement with your tenants, you must first have a lease agreement for everyone to sign. The first thing you are going to need to determine, is the length of the lease that you are going to commit to. The two most common agreements are month to month agreements, and one-year leases. Most landlords are going to choose the one-year lease option, as this allows them to keep tenants in the home as long as possible and minimize turnover. Regardless of the timeframe you choose to go with for your lease agreement, you want to ensure that it is stated clearly in your lease. Then everyone is on the same 'page.'

While lease agreements can vary in length and content, most are going to contain the same basic information. This information includes:

- The names of the tenants.
- The address of the rental property.
- The length of the lease term.
- The amount of the security deposit.
- A description of the late fees.
- The move in condition report.
- Specific provisions regarding: pets, number of persons, utility inclusions, smoking, etc.

There may also be some state or federal documents that you are required to include in your lease agreement; so be sure to look into that, before you finalize what your tenants are signing. Be informed and organized, always.

Signing The Lease

When it comes to signing the lease, you will want to make sure that it is done correctly. Meeting with the tenant at the property (to fill out the move-in report and sign the lease), is the most common way to ensure this is done.

When you meet with the tenant, ensure that you go through the lease, section by section, and have them initial that they have agreed, on every point or paragraph. This is time-consuming, but it will protect you if, in the future, your tenant tries to say they weren't aware of a provision that is in the lease. This process is absolutely necessary, to cover you, as a landlord.

The Move in Report

The move in report is simply a piece of paper that documents exactly what the condition of the house is, when the tenant moves in. This is to protect you as well as the tenant. This is your chance to document every hole, stain, and missing door knob. When the tenant moves out - you and your tenant can do the same thing for a move-out report and compare the two to determine what repairs your tenant is responsible for.

Accepting Rent

You are going to want to ensure that you and your tenant are on the same page when it comes to how rent can be paid, and what happens if rent is paid late. You can choose how you want to accept rent, but as a general rule, most landlords choose to get the funds in the form of a cashier's check or money order. You can also accept personal checks, but ensure that you have a clause in the lease, so you are protected, if the check doesn't clear, as an example. Ensure that you are providing receipts to your tenants for their rent. Use a diary and a file folder to keep track of payments and receipts.

You can go to your rental property every month to collect your rent; this gives you the chance to glance in and make sure that things are looking like they are being taken care of. However, this is going to mean that you need to go to the property and connect with your tenant.

How you choose to collect your rent is up to you, and you can change or adapt how you are doing it as time passes, and you may also learn more about your tenant and what the commitment level from you is going to be.

Once your tenant has filled out the lease, and it has been signed, and the rent has been paid, you can hand over the keys and allow them possession. This is when you are finally able to reap the benefits of all the work you have put into getting the property. You can finally start collecting a passive income from it.

Managing Your Rentals

Managing a property can be a really stressful experience, but also a rewarding one. Whilst hiring a property manager can seem like the easier and more convenient way to lease a property and reap the benefits, managing your own rentals isn't actually as tough as you might think.

First of all, maintaining professionalism is a must! Becoming too friendly with your tenant could lead to some hidden disasters. So, while it's vital to have a positive relationship, it doesn't necessary have to be a friendship. This will become more evident if the tenant is late supplying their rent and if they consider you more of a friend. Also, be professional (not too friendly), as they're less likely to pay you with the cash as soon as it is due. This is a business arrangement, after all. No friendship is advisable.

Benefits of self-management

Less expensive

This is important if you are just starting out on your property managing journey. Property managers and their companies will charge fees for their services, so doing plenty of research on the most equipped and recommended companies could help you find the right manager, quickly.

More involved

You can be as involved as you want if you're doing it all yourself! From picking the tenant to sorting out rental agreements; everything you want from the experience is yours to handle. For some, this might seem a little daunting whilst for others it's a dream come true! By being more involved from the start, you will learn a lot more than if you hired someone else to do it for you. So, in the future when you want to add to your real estate portfolio - you won't be so out of your depth or comfort zone.

You are in control

That means if you dislike a tenant or wish to raise the rent, you can do that! It also means that you have to deal with everything from late rent to neighbor disputes, which can become a little bit overwhelming. But once you have the right information, you can't go wrong!

Other important factors to keep in mind is doing adequate research on the legal aspect of managing your own rental property. Each state has different legislation, to protect both the tenant and owner. So, being up to date with the what is allowed and not allowed in your particular state, will save you trouble later on. If you're a little stuck on where to start, you could always contact a local property manager and ask for some general advice. If they think you're already struggling, they might think you will consult them later on how to manage the property.

Once you've settled on a tenant, forming a binding leasing agreement and bond arrangement will be your next step. And whilst you might think you know exactly what goes into these types of legal documentations, it is always best to consult a professional. Having a 'go-to' lawyer is vital; one you can trust and know will always try their best to help you out. Forming a solid relationship with them early, could potentially pay off in the long run.

Benefits of using a property manager

So, if you have ultimately come to the conclusion that self-managing a property just isn't for you, there are plenty of options available to you! Having a property manager means you don't have to deal with the day to day issues surrounding managing a property. Here are a few benefits of going with a property manager:

- **They will market the property for you.** Unless you're a marketing guru, you will most likely use some of the top real

estate renting websites to attract potential tenants, which is fine! Property managers on the other hand, will spend time researching demographics and rental prices to ensure your property is rented out, quickly.
- *Any tenant issues are dealt with by them.* If there is an issue with payment or breaking the contract, you won't have to go through the messy process of handling and sorting out the situation. They will do this on your behalf.
- *It is their job to show the client the property.* This essentially means no more of your own Saturdays will be spent waiting on people - to turn up and view your property!
- *They tend to have a better screening process for tenants.* This doesn't necessarily mean that you can't screen them yourself adequately, but it does mean that they have a lot more experience dealing with troublesome tenants. And so they almost have a radar for what makes a 'bad' tenant. Screening processes help to cull out time wasters and non-genuine individuals.
- *Increasing your property value.* If you are planning on selling the property at some point (whether it be in a year or five years); if the property has been managed, it tends to add a bit more appeal to your property value, exponentially.
- *Opens up more investment opportunities.* If you like to think of yourself as a savvy investor, hiring a property manager means it frees up your time to spend looking or renovating a new property.
- *They're not attached to the property.* If the home you're trying to rent out is one that you love and cherish, it's going to be hard to hear that one of the tenants has destroyed the carpet, or that the unapproved dog chewed up the floorboards. So, unless this is purely an investment property - you don't have a personal attachment to it. So, it's going to be difficult to self-manage your property, if you are attached. It is not impossible though!

While hiring a property manager is convenient, it can be a little expensive so make sure you do your research before committing to anything! If you own a property that is managed by a Strata company, self-managing a property can be quite difficult if you're not sure of the restrictions and guidelines given to the apartment or condominium. It's times like this having a property manager would actually be very useful.

Chapter 11: The Rehabilitation of Rental Properties

The purpose behind a privately organized rental rehabilitation program, is to enhance the well-being, respectability, transparency and curbside marketability of the owned investment property. In addition, the rehabilitation should be occurring between tenancies, where possible. This is highly recommended, to ensure: sustainable quality standards, code requirement adhesions, additional attractiveness, and the best possible rent achievable, within the locality.

The execution of a rehabilitation incorporation, assists the owner of properties, to achieve substantial improvements, within their rental facilities. The rehabilitation phase usually allows for: required repairs on the interior and/or exterior, improvements of energy and water efficiencies, environmental efficacy (like asbestos and lead plants), and remodeling for livability improvements, too.

In order to gain the benefits, the investment should be a low-to-moderate income property, in most cases. The entrepreneur (you), will be able to claim the expenditure for improvements for taxation purposes, with their accountant too.

In order to be well organized, the project for remodeling and rehabilitation is arranged to occur in between tenancies, and this is to allow for as little disruption as possible of tenants, and is set to meet the various requirements planned out by you. These will differ from property to property. Ideally, the work (if carried out by contractors) will be pre-arranged for a set date. This will enable the shortest possible time frame (without rental income), to occur.

As indicated, there may be other factors that will be considered too, including; the type of building being rehabilitated, and the all-important 'budget conscious,' economic feasibility. The property should be of sound structure and need repairs or improvements that are: acceptable to maintain code requirements for standards, as well as being visually appealing to tenants, on a 'great looks' basis.

The investor, therefore, always needs to improve the property when possible. This ensures the constant, competitive marketability, and the mandatory code adherence requirements, as well. Some great added advice is to keep the building simple including: similar colorings throughout, hard floors, minimal carpeting, effective lighting, appliance additions and easy to maintain wet areas. Easy maintenance gardens and grounds are advisable, too.

Chapter 12: The Four Core Exiting Strategies

Hold Forever

Hold forever can also refer to the buy and hold strategy. This is an investment strategy where entrepreneurs purchase a stock, and keep them for a long time. The major idea in hold forever is the concept of day trading, in which you are able to make money in the short term, and if we try to avoid buying in peaks, instead, we buy on low seasons. If warranted the owner will sell on the peaks; hence money coming with greater volatility.

Let me say that this idea is actually based on the perception that we always have; that long run financial markets give a good rate of return, even when considering the degree of volatility. So, it also outlines that the buyer might never gain those returns if they bail out after a decline. From this viewpoint, I understand that market timing is not predictable, and that one can have a perception that the product is cheap; only for the prices of the product to fall much lower in the future.

Passive management is common in the equity market, since index funds track a stock market index. Other sectors such as bonds, commodities and hedge funds are adopting the idea of tracking the index funds hence increasing the hold forever strategy. Barclay's Global Investors and State Street Corporation, largely use the passive management strategy.

On the contrary, the efficient-market hypothesis (EMH), where if the securities are fairly based at all times then there is no point for trading. Still, the owner experiences other hindrances, such as brokerage and bid/offer spread on all contracts. And the buy-and-hold theory includes the least transaction for a given venture. Taxation benefits are included in the buy-and-hold policy. This is because tax for long-term investment capital may be substantially lower, and the investor incurs the taxes at the time of sale only.

Seller Financing

This is an agreement between the seller and the buyer; where the seller lends the buyer money for the purchase, instead of the buyer getting a loan from the bank. They come up with a promissory note that describes the terms and conditions of the transaction, which includes the payment plan, interest rate and the penalties for nonpayment.

Let us look at this together, and so if the real estate market is not functioning that well; disasters are numerous - such as difficulties in getting bank loans. The credit market is still in hangover mode and a 'throbbing headache.' Sellers are working out strategies to get the highest possible price for their properties while the short sales, depreciations and tight credit market are blocking the market. The seller financing is benefiting to the buyer since it is an investment, with a guaranteed return by the buyer as the ability to pay the mortgage. While for the buyer it is a great deal since he/she may not be able to obtain a loan from the bank.

Since there are no universal requirements mandate for seller financing, a purchase agreement facilitates the protection of the buyer and seller interests. An attorney assists in the drawing of the agreement. This occurs before the buyer and the seller sign the agreement. The buyer does not receive the legal documents such as the legal title to the property until he/she pays fully, the total mortgage. While seller financing provides a unique way for people with low credit scores to own a property, bigger firms consider it predatory and fear being involved in the idea, for negative reputation attraction.

Cash-out Strategy

Cash-out is also the exit strategy. It is a contingency plan by an entrepreneur to liquidate a financial position in an asset, or dispose of properties when it has achieved an objective or exceeded criteria. We use the cash-out strategy to close a firm that is not performing, or for a firm that no longer generates profit. This is to ensure that we reduce liabilities encountered. A business that has met the main objective can also be exited, or venture into other business to re-establish the same business with new objectives and strategies.

Other causes can be the significant change in the market due to catastrophic happenings, legal reforms or the owner's decision to cash-out. Maybe since he/she is retiring. The plan of the cash-out should consider both benefits and consequences of the exit, and should also determine the effects associated with the investment or business, as well.

During business, venture entrepreneurs always plan for a comprehensive cash-out strategy in case of a failure to achieve the set goals. When the cash sales are no longer sustainable (and external capital funding is no longer enough to maintain the business in operation), the investor opts to terminate the operation and liquefy all assets, to avoid more losses. The entrepreneurs may decide to exit if another party gives a very lucrative offer. Also, in the context of a trading, the cash-out strategy assists traders with controlling their emotions when trading; to avoid lustful acts of leaving a business, to venture into a more profiting scheme. And which might lead to losing.

The 1031 Exchange

1031 exchange is a section of the United States internal revenue service code. It gives investors a chance to defer capital gains taxes on assets, especially the like-kind properties, for business or investment reasons. There is a tax exemption on the sales of the properties if the money earned is for re-investment purposes. The main idea here is that when you sell a property and purchases a similar one, you will have no economic gain. The tax exemption and exclusion strategies can effectively reposition your property to accomplish financial objectives; avoiding income tax liabilities.

This platform has various benefits - such as tax exemption including ordinary income, capital gain, depreciation recapture and Medicare surcharge admissions. These payments will reduce your capital, hence making it difficult to reinvest in larger and more profitable properties.

You also benefit from lifetime exchanging by increasing your net worth faster; throughout your lifetime, as you continually defer the income tax liabilities.

You also gain from the step-up cost basis; this means that your heirs will get a step up cost that is equal to the fair market value. This is true for your investment at the time of your death, and they can sell the property immediately, (free from capital gain and depreciation that recaptures income tax liabilities).

The strategy has various structures such as; simultaneous 1031 exchange that enables you to swap the properties and the transactions, all closing on the same day. A delayed 1031 exchange gives you a chance to sell your property, then acquire another within the prescribed period. The reverse 1031 exchange gives you a chance to purchase your replacement property, before selling the relinquished property.

Chapter 13: Extra Information and Terms

Choosing where to buy is the most important decision an investor makes. This is the best advice in the book, actually! For the property owner, deciding some other important factors is also paramount to successful investment. Here they are:

Evaluation

Just as I have stated above, choosing the right place to buy is the most important job for a successful investor. Yes, the neighborhood needs to be a 'good' place. Importantly, it is the duty of a potential investor to investigate the neighborhood of a property where they want to purchase. This investigation is mostly to ensure that this neighborhood respects various standards, and preferences of the potential tenant. Mostly, preferences such as safety, sanity and other basic needs, and also the availability of warranted education (like schools and colleges). We have touched on this before, however, it is actually a very imperative choice. So we are reminded of it again, 'on purpose.'

Calculations

Most probably, the second most important factor to look at before leasing for tenancy, is the overall cost of doing so. This includes the total rental price achievable, first-period deposits, and other minor fees in accordance with the tenancy terms, such as insurances, utilities etc. Prior knowledge of these costs before making the lease helps with the cost and bill calculations – before the lease is signed.

Landlord Policies

Although landlords should not discriminate against a certain class of individuals in the society, it is their duty to select their prospective tenants according to their behaviors, character traits, and virtual day-to-day habits. Therefore, landlords are free to apply various rules regarding pets, smoking and other policies; as long as they are not discriminating against prospective individuals. In addition, another major policy in tenancy is about rent and fee payment. It is a duty of a landlord to reject or cast-off prospective tenants' inability to pay rent, and other transactional fees, according to the terms of the tenancy agreement therein. Be thorough in your lease, and cover...everything.

Reputation Information

Information about the tenant's reputation is also an important factor before leasing. Arguably, online reputation and previous tenancies are great sources of information regarding professional, personal and overall character traits of prospective tenants. Therefore, you should talk and always look for the current or prior imperative additional information.

By-Advantages

By-advantages are the side advantages a tenant may acquire from the tenancy program, such as security, parking and other significances to a tenant. Major aids - such as insurance, also better the tenancy program. This is the reason behind renters buying renter's insurance after a lease. Make sure that renters have insurance or an insurance policy that covers a renter's belongings, in case of accidents such as fire. Considering the clauses behind these insurance policies is also a factor to look at before leasing. This helps the tenants to realize more advantages from the insurance policies, too. Landlords and property owners should ensure their tenant/s have insurance, as part of the lease terms, exponentially. As a landlord you may add this clause into the tenancy, for added peace of mind. Add some benefits like private parking where possible. This will be a great attraction for long term tenants, who will really enjoy the extra benefits.

Important Definitions/Terms

AMORTIZATION is the paying loans with a fixed repayment schedule in regular installments, over a period of time.

CREDIT is the trust that allows one party to provide resources to another party; where that second party repay or return those resources later.

CREDIT SCORE is a numerical expression based on a level analysis of a person's credit files, to represent his credit worthiness.

COMMERCIAL PROPERTY is the physical or intangible entity owned by a person or group of people, that is used solely for business purposes such as office buildings and retail stores.

DEPOSIT MORTAGE is a portion of funds that is used as a security or collateral for the delivery of goods.

INDUSTRIAL PROPERTY are inventions, industrial designs; trademark protected under national and international intellectual property laws.

IRS is the Internal Revenue Service known as a bureau of the department of treasury in the United States. And that enforces income tax laws, and oversees the collection of federal income taxes and determines pension plan qualifications.

LANDLORD is the person who leases his properties to tenants for real estate living or aboding.

MORTAGE is a conveyance of or lien against a property, that becomes void upon payment.

PROPERTY is the physical or intangible entity owned by an investor or a group of people.

RENT is a tenant's regular payment to a property owner for the express use of property or land.

RENTAL LEASE is a specified contract between a tenant and property owner, that defines the terms and conditions of the tenancy agreement.

RESIDENTIAL PROPERTY is a type of a non-business property available for an occupation, that may contain multifamily and/or single family structures.

RETAIL PROPERTY is a type of commercial property available for leasing to stores, service businesses and/or shopping centers.

SECURITY DEPOSIT/BOND is a sum of money held in trust; either as an initial part-payment, or in a purchasing process to secure the item or property denoted.

TENANT a person who occupies land or property rented from a property owner or landlord.

UTILITIES are the elements to be used to live in a property or dwelling. Including: electricity, gas, water and sewage.

Chapter 14: The Fundamentals of Being a Successful Property Investor/Manager

When it comes to picking a property for rental investment, it can be a little bit tricky when you're first dipping your toes into the market. So, here are certain things to look out for when finding a rental investment property. Some of the top property characteristics to look out for are mentioned below. We have touched on some of these earlier…but it is important to be clear, now.

What type of investment do you want to manage?

- Free standing family homes
- Townhouses
- Duplexes
- Small Apartment buildings/units
- Standard apartment buildings with more than two levels
-

Once you've found which location is going to work for you, next comes figuring out whether or not the property is the right fit for you. Things to consider when analyzing a property include:

- Is there any structural damage to the property?
- How much maintenance and upkeep is required (e.g. is there a pool or tennis court?)
- Does it require any renovations or painting to make it ready for a tenant?
- If it's in an apartment building, what is the building like?

Deciding what real estate agent or company you want to go with, is another issue first time investors struggle with. A few important traits you want your real estate team to have are:

- They come highly recommended.
- Do they have good feedback from clients?
- Positive mindset is obvious.
- Determined to work hard.
- Strong communication skills.
- Proactive in business dealings.
- Assertive and self-confident.
- Client motivated and professional.
- They happily give you their last clients as referees.

- They understand your needs and time frame.
- They make you feel comfortable and important.

Three tips for getting your loan application approved:

1. Have a strong credit history and credit score.
2. Have a substantial amount saved already.
3. You can show consistency with your work/employment.

After your initial application, waiting to be approved can be stressful - but by ensuring you have all your bases covered, this will help speed up the process. Here are a few tips to help you close the deal:

- Have all the necessary paperwork ready.
- Be honest with your bank or lender, if you had to default on a loan in the past – let them know.
- Use pre-approvals to help move the process along, more quickly.

Not only is being a landlord a great way to earn passive income, it's also rewarding mentally and emotionally. Unlike a lot of other ways to increase your cash flow - being a landlord will mean you are constantly learning and developing, and what's not to love about that?

It can be tricky at first to navigate the sometimes confusing world of the real estate property market. But once you have a fair understanding of what it takes to be a good landlord; soon enough it'll be second nature to you! One of the major benefits of becoming a landlord is that you will be consistently bringing in a steady amount of passive income. Along with that, over time the property will also appreciate in value, and progressively increase your capital worth. In order to get there though, there are a few fundamentals to be aware of:

- **_Have a number of trusty tradespeople on call._**
There for those emergencies that you never expect to arise. Managing unplanned incidents like a gas leak or broken window and reacting to the issues swiftly. This will not only make you a reliable landlord but by keeping your tenants happy, you'll also benefit, as well. If, however, you end up being the type of landlord that leaves problems until they become major issues; you'll find it difficult to keep tenants, long term.

- ***Sort out every single legal issue imaginable.*** From the building insurance to a rock solid rental agreement; make sure you are covered for anything that could potentially come up. It's especially important if your property is in a particularly dangerous, too. Always consult a lawyer before undertaking such a massive step like being a landlord; find out your rights as the property owner as it can differ dramatically, from state to state.
- ***Don't underestimate what goes into being a great landlord.*** From handling neighbour squabbles to organising maintenance work. And although it is a passive way to earn income, it can end up feeling like more of a part time job. This is especially obvious at the beginning when the screening and inspection stage can seem as though it goes on forever. There can also be unexpected legal costs if things with the tenants become strained. And this is one of the main reasons you need to be aware of your legal rights and responsibilities. Be patient and learn everything you can about property management in the meantime. Always back everything up with great knowledge. Look at the legalities first, before you start. The say, "knowledge is power."
- ***It can be a little bit addictive.*** Once you have your first property under your belt, you may soon feel like moving onto your second or even third property! Just keep in mind that this will also entail even more expenses. For example, a home office, mortgages, expenditures and renovation costs.
- ***Managing finances.*** If you aren't the best at keeping track of spending, then you might want to consider an accountant. A great tip is with the rent money the tenants provide you with, most of it would obviously go to paying a mortgage off. And whatever is left over, keep aside for emergency maintenance or utility costs, as required. You could even save ten percent of your rent, long term.

Conclusion

Now that you are aware of the steps that are going to be involved in obtaining a property, (and using it to generate passive income), you are ready to get started.

You should feel confident that you can approach this process with the knowledge you need to be successful. Successful at finding not only a rental property, but also a suitable tenant - to ensure that you are creating income, and not sitting on an empty rental property investment.

Your next step after reading this book and deciding this venture is for you:

Are going to be able to get your financing and find your property? Before you know it you are going to be well on your way to building your rental property empire.

I would like to thank you again for downloading my book, *Real Estate Investing:*
The Ultimate Wealth Guide to Rental Property Investing, Real Estate & Passive Income.

I hope it has provided you with all of the information that you were looking for - as well as some information you didn't know you needed, too!

Wishing you much luck and success in your passive investment income future…

Finally, if you enjoyed this book, would you be kind enough to leave a review for this book on Amazon? It'd be greatly appreciated! Thank you so much!

www.ingramcontent.com/pod-product-compliance
Lightning Source LLC
Chambersburg PA
CBHW070356190526
45169CB00003B/1031